Imagine and Draw

Baxter loves to take his skateboard for a spin.
Who is skateboarding with him in the park? Draw them here.

Hidden Pictures® Doodle

Mike, Cara, and Sam are painting a poster for their basketball team.
What do you think they are painting? Help them design the poster. Then try to find the
hidden ruler, hockey puck, fork, crescent moon, baseball bat, and ring.

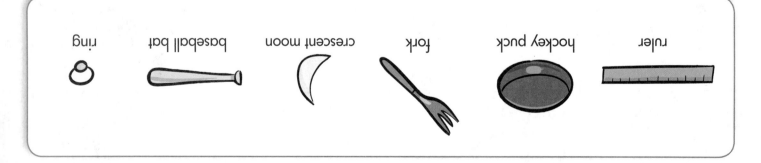

ring

baseball bat

crescent moon

fork

hockey puck

ruler

Hide It!

Can you hide this wedge of orange in
your own Hidden Pictures® drawing?
We gave you some ideas in these pictures.

Build a Bot

Draw this robot some legs.

Draw this robot a head.

Draw this robot some arms.

Step by Step

Follow the steps to draw an elephant, or draw one from your imagination.

1. 2. 3.

Draw Your Elephant in a Scene

Now that you've practiced drawing elephants, draw them in the scene below, or draw some of your favorite animals.

What Is It?

Create a drawing by using these lines as a starting point.
What could it be? A grapefruit? A flower? A window to a house?

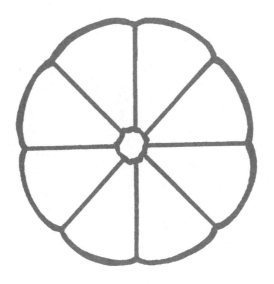

Imagine and Draw

These cows see something surprising on top of the fence.
What do you think they are looking at? Draw it here.

Alphabet Animals

Did you know you can draw a swan using the letter "S"?
Follow these steps to learn how!

1.

2.

3.

Hidden Pictures® Doodle

Knight class is in session! Professor Knightingale is teaching his class a lesson. Draw what you think he is showing them. Then try to find the hidden magnet, paper clip, ax, telescope, handbag, ladle, drumstick, mushroom, and hairbrush.

Answers

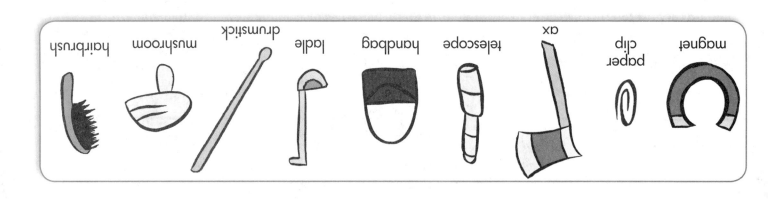

magnet

paper clip

ax

telescope

handbag

ladle

drumstick

mushroom

hairbrush

Hide It!

Can you hide this banana in
your own Hidden Pictures® drawing?
We gave you some ideas in these pictures.

Cartooning a Face

Here are some ideas on how to begin cartooning a face. First, draw a face shape, like a circle or an oval. Then play around with some different hairstyles. Now you give it a try!

What's Hiding?

What is that hiding under the bed? Draw what you think it is.

A-maze-ing!

These skaters are soaring! At the end of each path, use your imagination to design a different ramp. Then follow the paths to see which ramp each skater is using to launch.

Imagine and Draw

Here is a shoe that you can design. Will it have a unique logo? What colors will you make it? Use your imagination to add some personal touches.

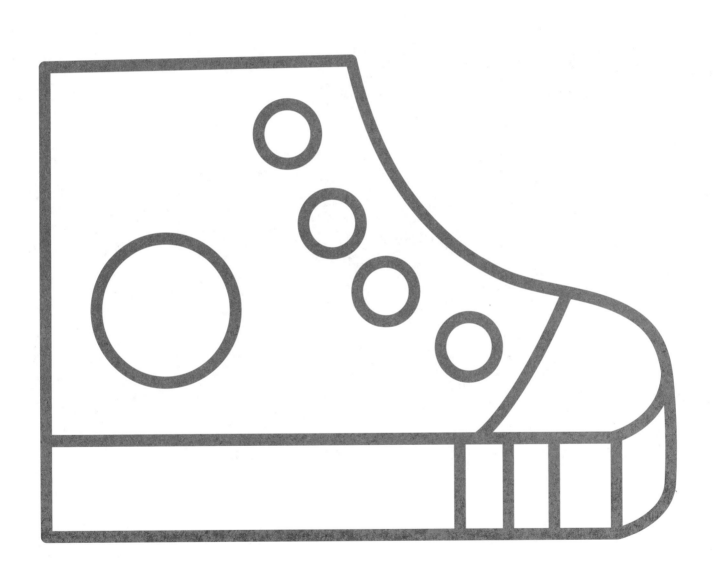

Hidden Pictures® Doodle

These birds are having a disco party! Who do you think is busting moves on the dance floor? Draw them in the scene here. Then try to find the wedge of orange, drinking straw, slice of pie, yo-yo, harmonica, and sailboat.

wedge of orange

drinking straw

slice of pie

yo-yo

harmonica

sailboat

Hide It!

Can you hide this boomerang in
your own Hidden Pictures® drawing?
We gave you some ideas in these pictures.

Build a Town

The town of Doodleton is expanding! What do you think it needs?
A library? A park? More houses and mailboxes? Draw your ideas inside the town.

FIR

Step by Step

Follow the steps to draw a spider, or draw one from your imagination.

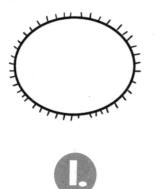

1.

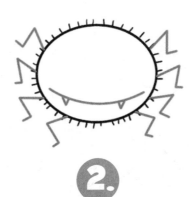

2.

3.

Draw Your Spider in a Scene

Now that you've practiced drawing spiders, draw them in the scene below, or draw some of your favorite critters.

What Is It?

Create a drawing using these lines as a starting point.
What could it be? A whale? A pool float?
A creature no one has ever seen before?

Imagine and Draw

The fireflies and stars are shining bright.
Follow the dots from 1 to 26 to see what picture the star constellation is making.
Then draw your very own star constellation.

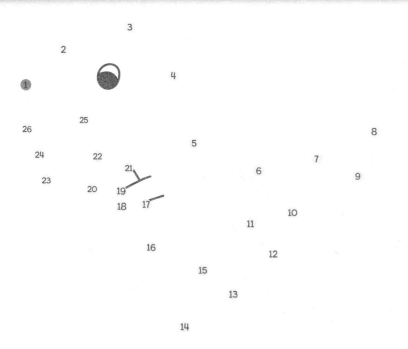

Animal Patterns

This zebra is missing her stripes! Can you draw in the rest of her stripes by following a pattern like the one on the other zebra?

Hidden Pictures® Doodle

Cats have taken over the playground!
What else are they doing? Draw it in below.
Then try to find 14 hidden mice in the picture.

Hide It!

Can you hide these glasses in
your own Hidden Pictures® drawing?
We gave you some ideas in these pictures.

Cartooning a Face

Add faces to these eyes, and then practice drawing eyes from your imagination.
Try drawing eyes with different expressions, like the ones here.

What's Hiding?

What is hiding in the tree? Draw what you think it is.

A-maze-ing!

Eric, Madison, Ashlyn, and Luke are wrapping presents.
Draw a present at the bottom of each ribbon below.
Then follow the ribbons to see who is wrapping each gift.

Imagine and Draw

Sam and Brittany are taking zoo selfies with a giraffe.
But someone—or something—photo-bombed their picture!
Who do you think sneaked into their picture? Draw them below.

Hidden Pictures® Doodle

Captain Banana-Split is setting sail on his next voyage. What do you think is painted on his ship's sails? Design the ship's sails below. Then try to find the hidden apple, ruler, open book, crayon, and scissors.

apple

 ruler

 open book

 crayon

 scissors

Answers

Hide It!

Can you hide the paper airplane in
your own Hidden Pictures® drawing?
We gave you some ideas in these pictures.

Build a Spaceship

Give this spaceship some wings.

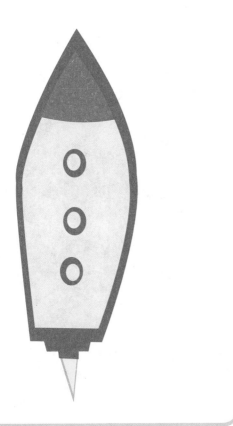

Draw the top of this spaceship.

Draw someone inside this spaceship.

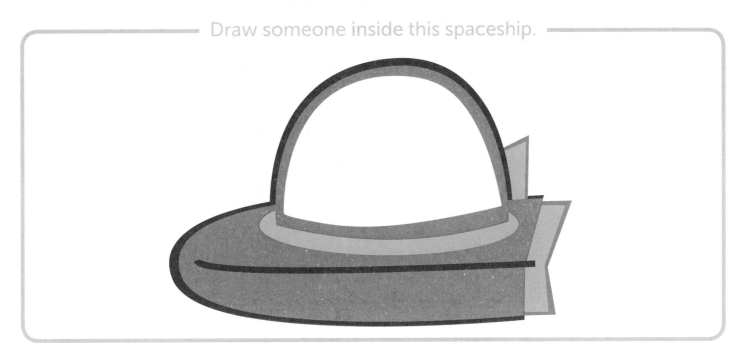

Step by Step

Follow the steps to draw a monster, or draw one from your imagination.

1. 2. 3.

Draw Your Monster in a Scene

Now that you've practiced drawing monsters, draw some in the silly scene below.

CAR WASH

9.5

What Is It?

Create a drawing by using these lines as a starting point.
What could it be? A cupcake? A T-shirt design? A face?

Imagine and Draw

Max hit a hole-in-one!
But something funny is hiding below the hole.
What do you think it is?

Alphabet Animals

Did you know you can draw a pig using the word "pig"?
Follow these steps to learn how!

1.

2.

3.

Hidden Pictures® Doodle

Jim the baker is taking out fresh pastries.
What do you think they look like? Draw them inside the case.
Then try to find the hidden garden hoe, snail, leaf, spool of thread, and birdhouse.

birdhouse

spool of thread

leaf

snail

garden hoe

Hide It!

Can you hide this sock in
your own Hidden Pictures® drawing?
We gave you some ideas in these pictures.

Cartooning a Face

Finish drawing the faces using these noses and mouths, and then practice drawing some of your own faces.

What's Hiding?

What is hiding in the seaweed? Draw what you think it is.

A-maze-ing!

Leaping Lizards! Larry got onto the roof.
Help him find his way back to the front door so he can get inside
where his friends are. Then draw Larry's animal friends in each window.

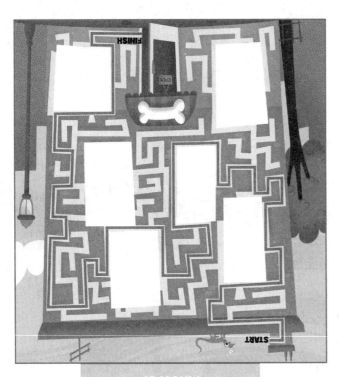

FINISH

OPEN

START

Answer

Imagine and Draw

Run, Sparky, run! What do you think Sparky the dog is chasing? Draw it here.

Hidden Pictures® Doodle

Everyone is having a blast in outer space! Draw what you think
is happening in this scene. Then try to find the hidden drinking glass,
slice of pie, banana, light bulb, slice of watermelon, flashlight, and coin.

 coin

 flashlight

 slice of watermelon

 light bulb

 banana

 slice of pie

 drinking glass

Answers

Hide It!

Can you hide this envelope in
your own Hidden Pictures® drawing?
We gave you some ideas in these pictures.

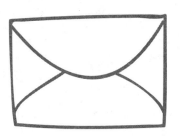

Build a Statue

Add a rider for
the horse.

Add the torch and crown
to the Statue of Liberty.

Draw your own statue on top of this marble base.

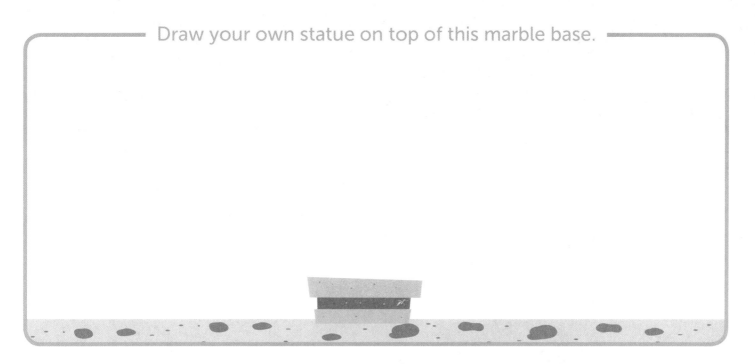

Step by Step

Follow the steps to draw a cat, or draw one from your imagination.

1.   2.   3.

Draw Your Cat in a Scene

Now that you've practiced drawing cats, draw them in the scene below, or draw some of your favorite animals.

What Is It?

Create a drawing using these lines as a starting point. What could it be?
A baby chick? A furry monster?

Imagine and Draw

What do you think John is drawing on the sidewalk?
Draw it below.

Animal Patterns

This leopard is missing his spots! Can you draw in the rest of his spots by following a pattern like the one on the other leopard?

Hidden Pictures® Doodle

What do you think is growing in the Jenkinses' garden?
Draw it in the picture below. Then try to find the hidden words:
BLOOM, DIG, VINE, and GARDEN.

Hide It!

Can you hide this piece of popcorn in
your own Hidden Pictures® drawing?
We gave you some ideas in these pictures.

Cartooning a Face

Here are some more ideas for cartooning faces.
Finish drawing faces around these accessories, or draw some of your own.

What's Hiding?

What is hiding in the bushes? Draw what you think it is.

A-maze-ing!

These squirrels are searching for nuts.
Draw a nut at the other end of each path,
and then follow the paths to see who will get which nut.

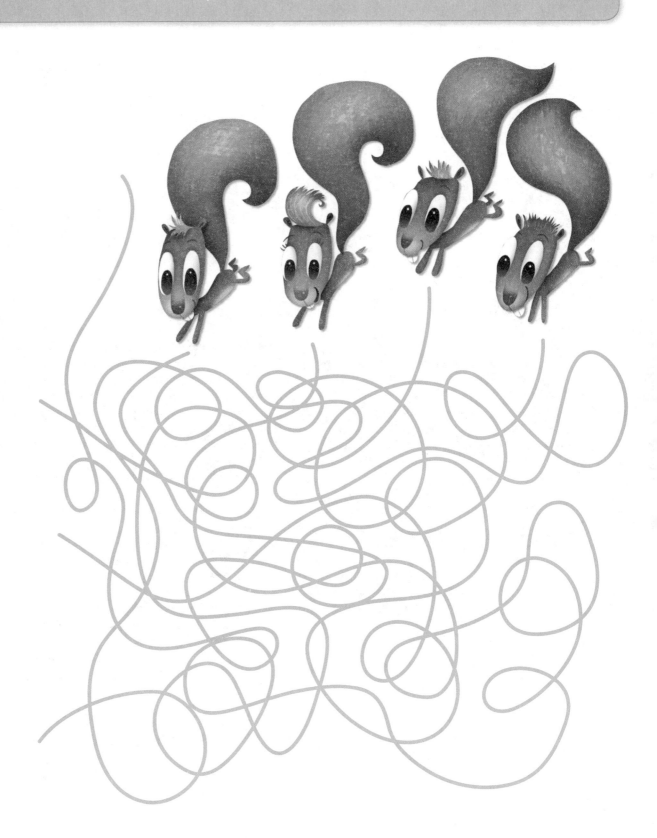

Imagine and Draw

Everyone is watching an amazing fireworks display.
What do you think the fireworks look like? Draw them in the sky.

Hidden Pictures® Doodle

Draw some wave-catching designs on Dillard's surfboard.
Then try to find the hidden lime, apple, banana, pear, and grapes.

Answers

grapes

pear

banana

apple

lime

Hide It!

Can you hide this fish in your own
Hidden Pictures® drawing?
We gave you some ideas in these pictures.

Build a Mascot

Give this
mascot a hat.

Draw something
on this mascot's flag.

Give this mascot some pom-poms.

Step by Step

Follow the steps to draw a castle, or draw one from your imagination.

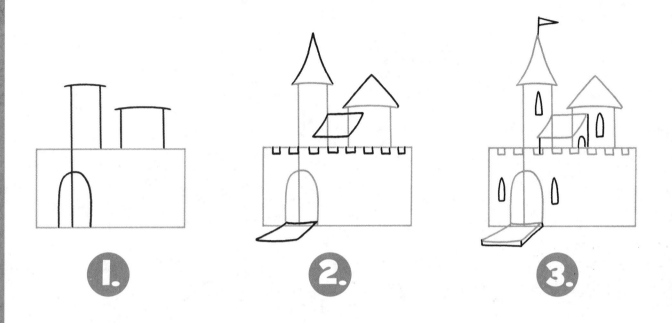

1.   **2.**   **3.**

Draw Your Castle in a Scene

Now that you've practiced drawing castles, draw one in the scene below.

What Is It?

Create a drawing using these lines as a starting point.
What could it be? A gate? A billboard? A unique pattern?

Imagine and Draw

Cindy is being carried away by the wind! What do you think is lifting her up so high in the sky? Draw what you think is on the other end of the string.

Alphabet Animals

Did you know you can draw a butterfly by drawing the letter "B"?
Follow these steps to learn how!

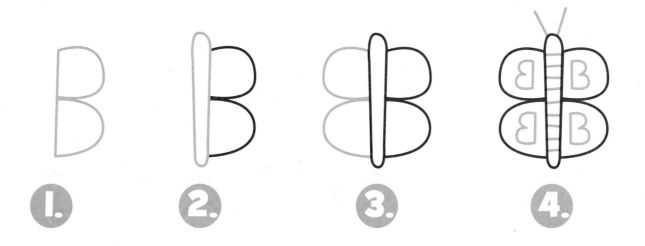

Hidden Pictures® Doodle

These penguins love to play on the ice. Draw some more penguins for them to play with. Then try to find the hidden slice of bread, tape dispenser, pear, slice of pizza, tack, spool of thread, and computer mouse.

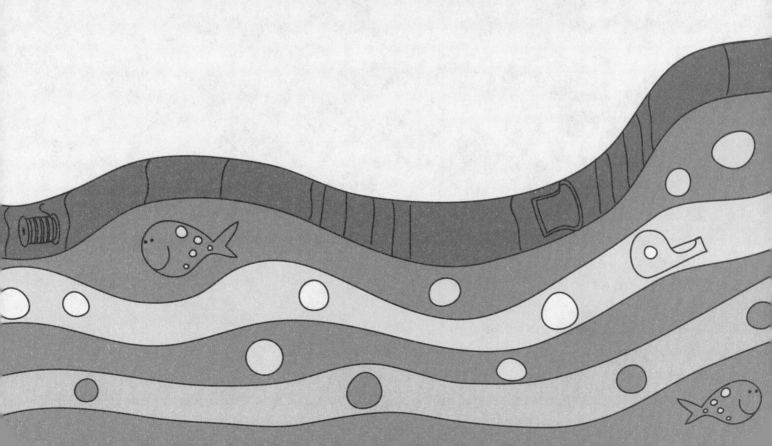

Answers

 computer mouse

 spool of thread

 tack

 slice of pizza

 pear

 tape dispenser

 slice of bread

Hide It!

Can you hide this crescent moon in
your own Hidden Pictures® drawing?
We gave you some ideas in these pictures.

Imagine and Draw

What do you think is inside this terrarium?
Turtles? Lizards? A garden? Draw it here.

What's Hiding?

What is hiding under the bridge? Draw what you think it is.

A-maze-ing!

These rock climbers got their ropes tangled. Can you set them straight? Draw a rope partner at the bottom of each rope, and then follow each rope, starting from the climber, to find out who his or her partner is.

Imagine and Draw

Here is a brand-new T-shirt for you to design!
Will your shirt have words or pictures, or both?

Hidden Pictures® Doodle

The ocean is full of surprises. What do you think is going on below the sea? Use your imagination to draw some creatures, plants, or maybe even treasure. Then try to find the hidden wedge of lime, tomato, trowel, slice of watermelon, crayon, and cinnamon roll.

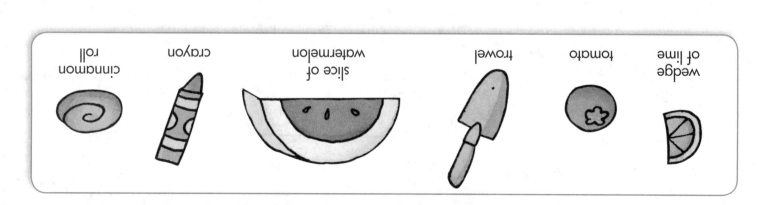

cinnamon roll

crayon

slice of watermelon

trowel

tomato

wedge of lime

Hide It!

Can you hide this yo-yo in
your own Hidden Pictures® drawing?
We gave you some ideas in these pictures.

Build a Monster

Add some arms
to this monster.

Add a body
to this monster.

Add some wings
to this monster.

Add a face
to this monster.

Step by Step

Follow the steps to draw a Tyrannosaurus rex, or draw one from your imagination.

Draw Your T. Rex in a Scene

Now that you've practiced drawing a T. rex, draw it in the scene below or draw some of your favorite dinosaurs.

What Is It?

Create a drawing using these lines as a starting point.
What could it be? A turtle? A turkey? An igloo?

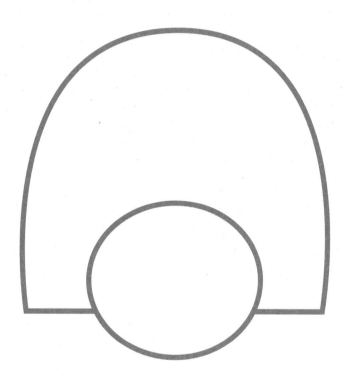

Imagine and Draw

This chair is a blank canvas. Design a pattern on the fabric—it can be simple or complex. What else do you think needs to go in the room? Draw it here.

Animal Patterns

This snake is missing his stripes and spots. Can you draw in the rest of his stripes and spots by making a pattern like the one on the other snake?

Hidden Pictures® Doodle

The traveling ants are putting on a hit show! Draw what you think is happening on the stage. Then try to find the hidden slice of pizza, fried egg, feather, seashell, cane, pie, and stick of gum.

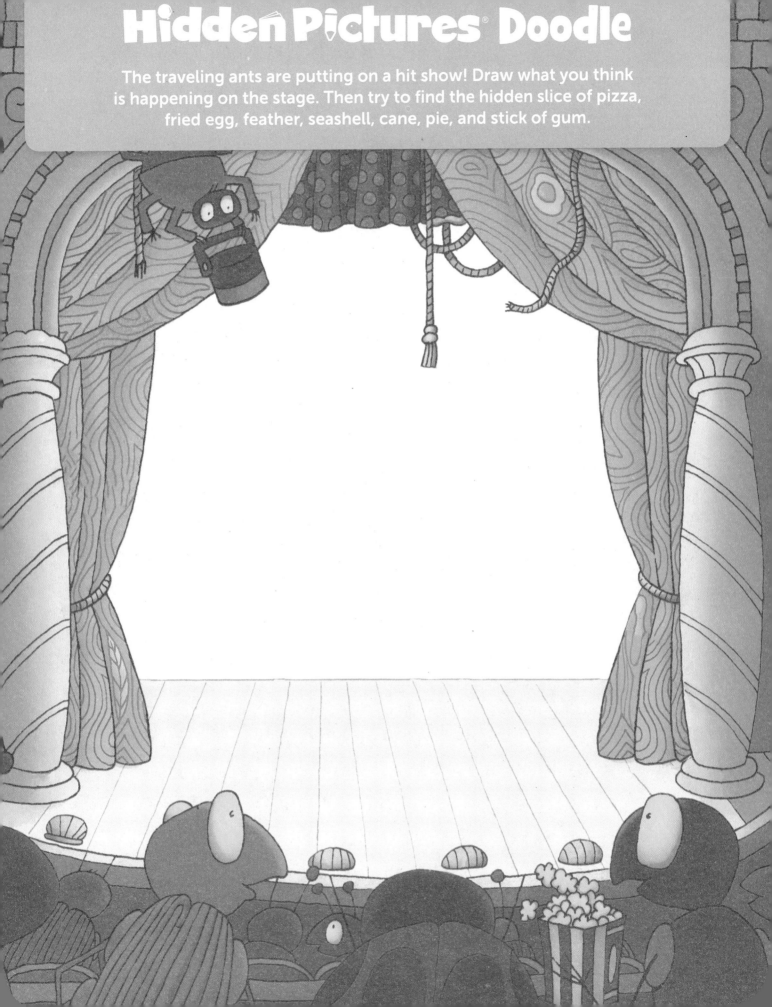

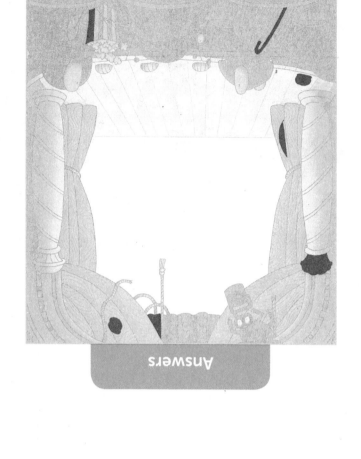

Answers

slice of pizza fried egg feather seashell cane pie stick of gum

Hide It!

Can you hide this pencil in
your own Hidden Pictures® drawing?
We gave you some ideas in these pictures.

Imagine and Draw

Fran and Fred are fishing on the lake. Is anything biting yet?
What else do you think is happening below their boat? Draw it here.

What's Hiding?

What is hiding behind the bookcase?
Draw what you think it is.

A-maze-ing!

These aliens need help finding their home planets. Draw a planet below each path, then follow the paths to see which planet belongs to which alien.

Imagine and Draw

This apartment building is filled with activity.
Draw what you think is happening inside each window.

Hidden Pictures® Doodle

Mike, Mary, and their dog Max are catching butterflies. Draw some nets they can use to catch the butterflies. Then try to find the hidden bow tie, raindrop, peanut, fork, egg, lollipop, snake, snowflake, and bowl.

Answers

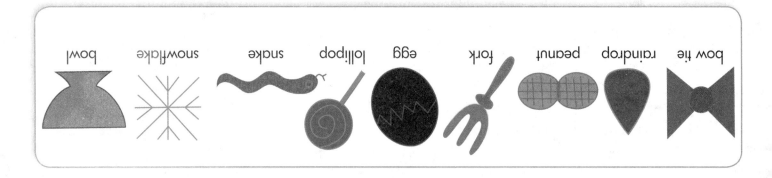

bow tie · raindrop · peanut · fork · egg · lollipop · snake · snowflake · bowl

Hide It!

Can you hide this crown in
your own Hidden Pictures® drawing?
We gave you some ideas in these pictures.

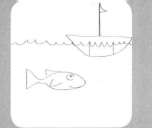

Build an Ice-Cream Creation

Add as many scoops to this cone as you want.

Add all your favorite flavors and toppings to this dish.

Now draw your own ice-cream creation!

Step by Step

Follow the steps to draw a giraffe, or draw one from your imagination.

1.   **2.**   **3.**   **4.**   **5.**

Draw Your Giraffe in a Scene

Now that you've practiced drawing giraffes, draw them in the scene below, or draw some of your favorite animals.

What Is It?

Create a drawing using these lines as a starting point.
What could it be? A jungle gym? A city skyline? A new invention?

Imagine and Draw

Kevin is writing a really imaginative story. What do you think it is about?
Draw a picture of a scene from his story.

Alphabet Animals

Did you know you can draw a dog using the word "dog"?
Follow these steps to learn how!

1.

2.

3.

Hidden Pictures® Doodle

Team Yellow hit it out of the park!
Draw the opposing team in a different color.
Then try to find the hidden paper airplane, skateboard, nail, ruler, pencil, and ladder.

Answers

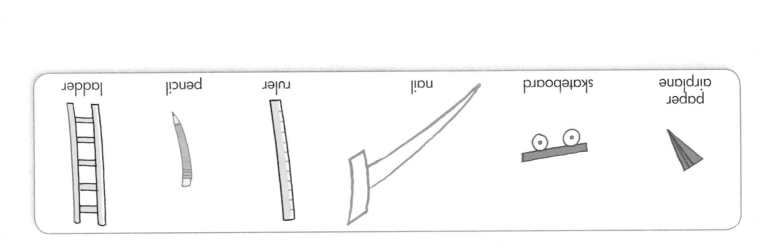

ladder

pencil

ruler

nail

skateboard

paper airplane

Hide It!

Can you hide this key in
your own Hidden Pictures® drawing?
We gave you some ideas in these pictures.

Imagine and Draw

Dr. Bacterio has just discovered something terribly exciting with her microscope. Draw what you think it is.

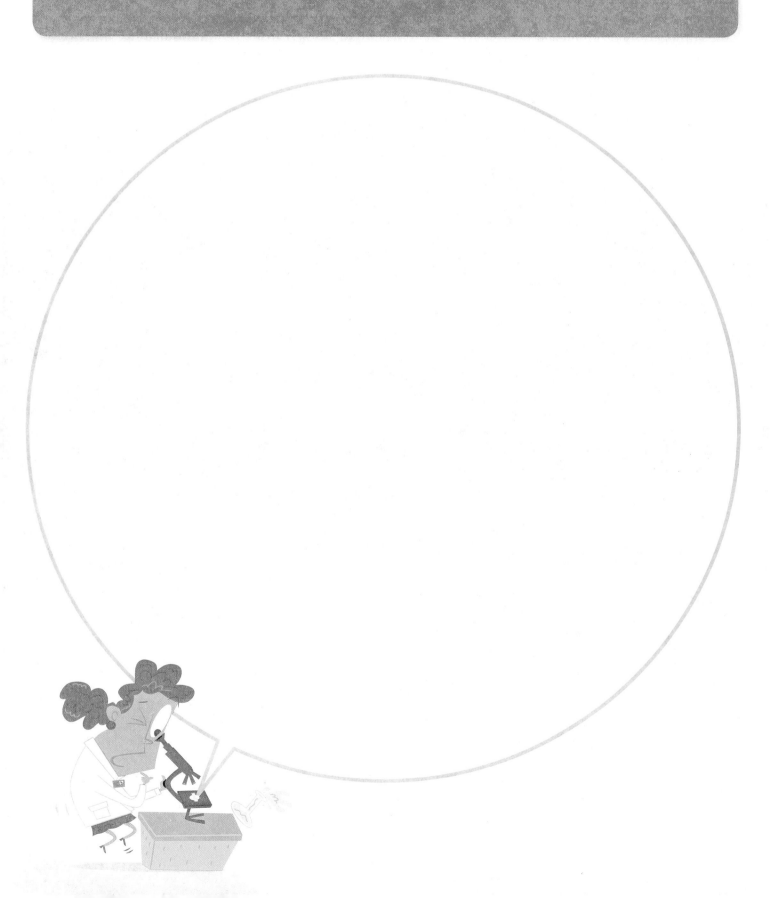

What Is It?

Create a drawing by using these lines as a starting point. What could it be? A scene under the ocean? A snapshot of ladybugs? A bouquet of flowers?

A-maze-ing!

These superheroes are ready to save the day. Draw someone—or something—for them to save at the end of each path, and then follow the paths to see who—or what—each superhero is going to save.

Imagine and Draw

Diana, Ralph, and Dave aren't the only ones floating down the river.
Who else do you think is taking a dip nearby? Draw them.

Hidden Pictures® Doodle

It's opening day at Teddy's Tacos. What else do you think should be added? Draw it here. Then try to find the hidden golf club, fork, button, glove, crescent moon, candle, doughnut, funnel, pencil, and hanger.

Answers

golf club

fork

button

glove

crescent
moon

candle

doughnut

funnel

pencil

hanger

Hide It!

Can you hide this top hat in
your own Hidden Pictures® drawing?
We gave you some ideas in these pictures.

Build a Bug

Draw shells on these snails.

Finish drawing the rest of this caterpillar.

Draw wings on these butterflies.

Step by Step

Follow the steps to draw an owl, or draw one from your imagination.

1. 2. 3. 4. 5.

Draw Your Owl in a Scene

Now that you've practiced drawing owls, draw them in the scene below, or draw some of your favorite animals.

What Is It?

Create a drawing using these lines as a starting point. What could it be?
A railroad track? A boardwalk? A neighborhood?

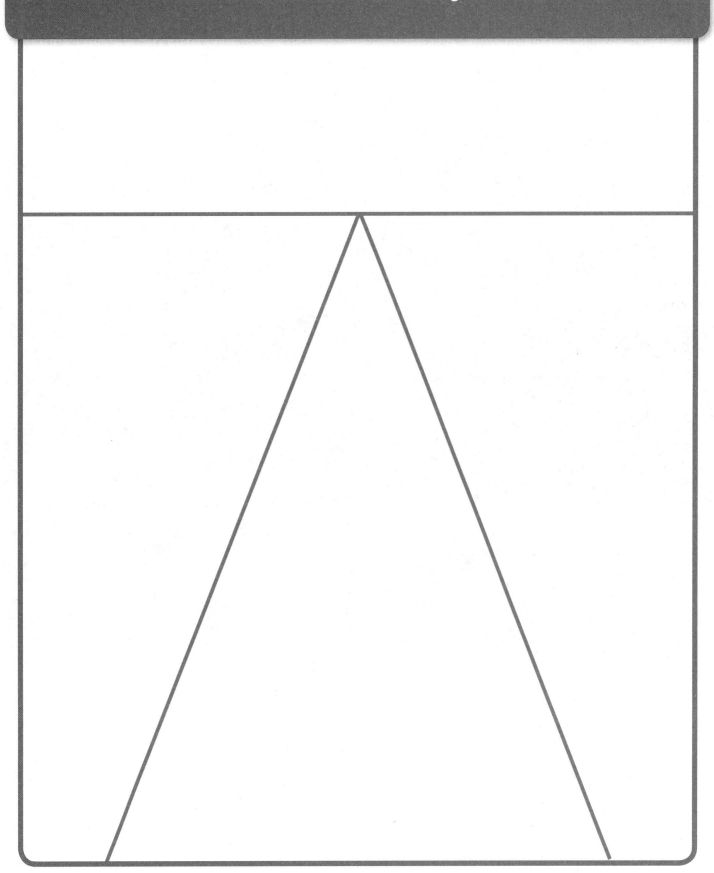

Imagine and Draw

Imagine you're getting your own book published.
What is your book called? How would you design the cover? Draw it here.

Alphabet Animals

Did you know you can draw a toucan using the letter "T"?
Follow these steps to learn how!

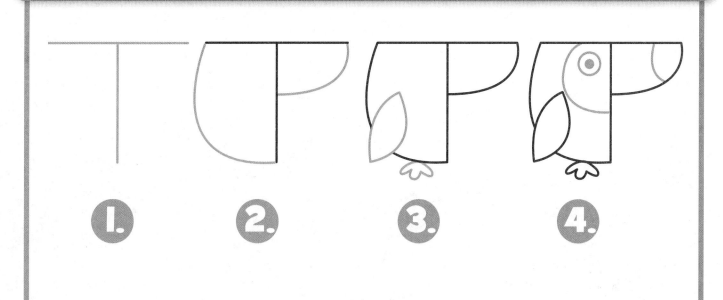

1. 2. 3. 4.

Hidden Pictures® Doodle

Who knew that moose were such great skiers! What else do you think is happening on the slopes? Draw it here. Then try to find the hidden saltshaker, needle, adhesive bandage, heart, paintbrush, wedge of orange, and drinking straw.

saltshaker   needle   adhesive bandage   heart   paintbrush   wedge of orange   drinking straw

Answers

Hide It!

Can you hide this sailboat in
your own Hidden Pictures® drawing?
We gave you some ideas in these pictures.

Imagine and Draw

What is Markus dreaming about?
Draw what you think he is dreaming here.

What's Hiding?

What is hiding inside the couch?
Draw what you think it is.

A-maze-ing!

These meerkats are about to head home. Draw what you think is inside their homes below each path. Then follow the paths to see which meerkat goes to which home.

Imagine and Draw

Chef Patisserie is making the most spectacular cake in the world!
Does it have 25 layers? Does it have stripes? Draw what you think it looks like.

Hidden Pictures® Doodle

This robot is taking his pet for a walk. What do you think his pet looks like?
What else do you think is happening at the park? Draw it in.
Then try to find the hidden button, envelope, pencil, sun, ruler, and book.

button
 envelope
 pencil
 sun
 ruler
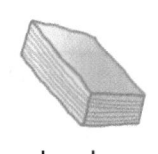 book

Answers

Hide It!

Can you hide this fork in
your own Hidden Pictures® drawing?
We gave you some ideas in these pictures.

Build a Pie

Finish the pies by drawing in the missing slices.

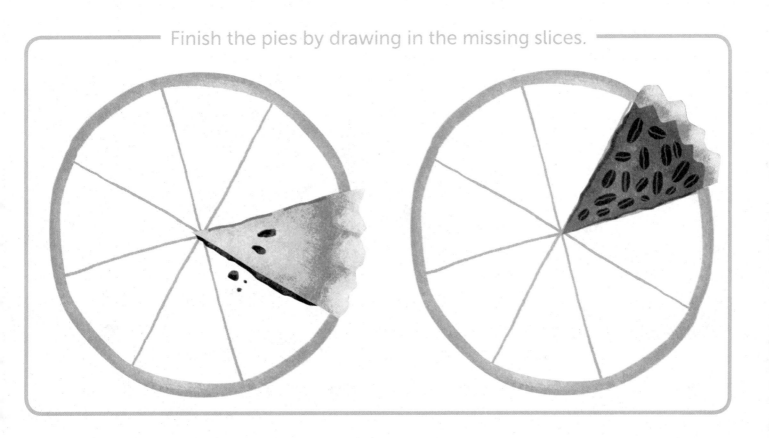

Draw your own pies! What flavors will they be?

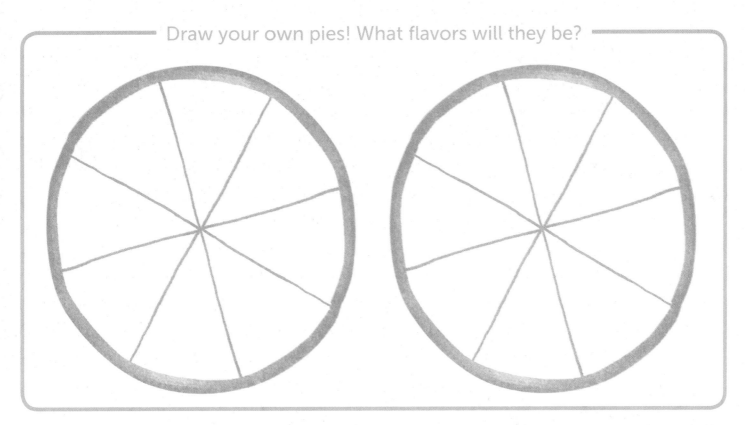

Step by Step

Follow the steps to draw a cow, or draw one from your imagination.

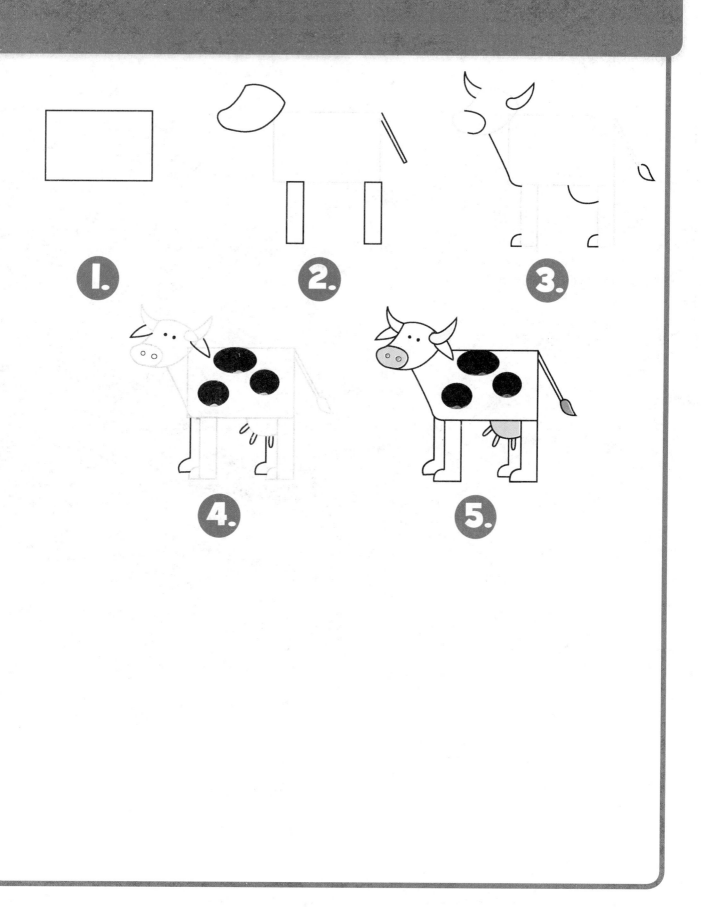

Draw Your Cow in a Scene

Now that you've practiced drawing cows, draw them in the scene below, or draw some of your favorite farm animals.

What Is It?

Create a drawing using these lines as a starting point.
What could it be? An umbrella? A spider web? A rainbow?

Imagine and Draw

The annual Homecoming Parade just rolled through town. This year's parade was filled with fantastic floats. What do you think the first-place float looked like? Draw it here.

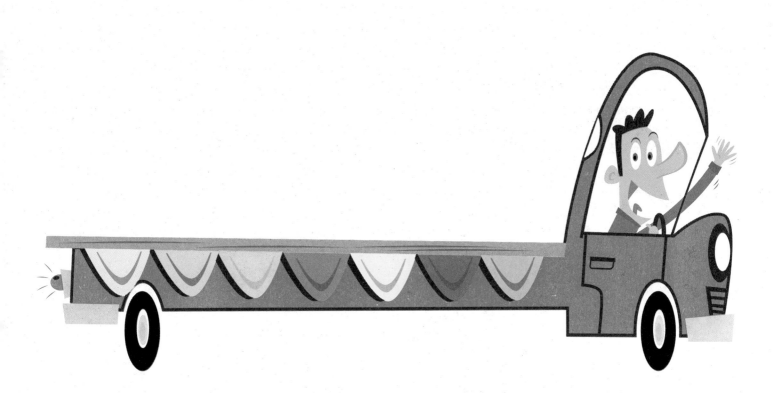

Animal Patterns

This peacock is missing the spots on his feathers.
Can you draw them in by following a
similar pattern on the other peacock?

Hidden Pictures® Doodle

These bunnies are soaring high! What else do you think is in the sky?
Draw it here. Then try to find the hidden flashlight, fish,
slice of pie, open book, and domino.

Answers

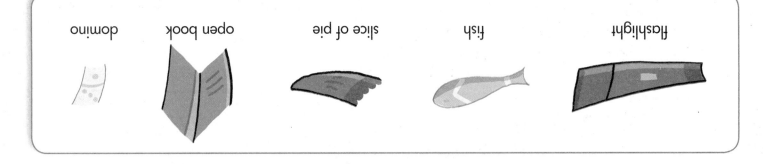

flashlight

fish

slice of pie

open book

domino

Hide It!

Can you hide this ice-cream cone in
your own Hidden Pictures® drawing?
We gave you some ideas in these pictures.

Build a Superhero

Draw this superhero a mask. What else does this superhero need?

Draw this superhero a logo on his shirt.

What is this superhero stopping? Finish the scene.

Art Gallery

Draw a unique piece of art on the blank canvas.

Art Gallery

Draw a self-portrait, or draw
something else from your imagination.

Art Gallery

Draw a picture of your dream pet, or
draw something else from your imagination.

Art Gallery

Draw a picture of your favorite memory, or draw something else from your imagination.

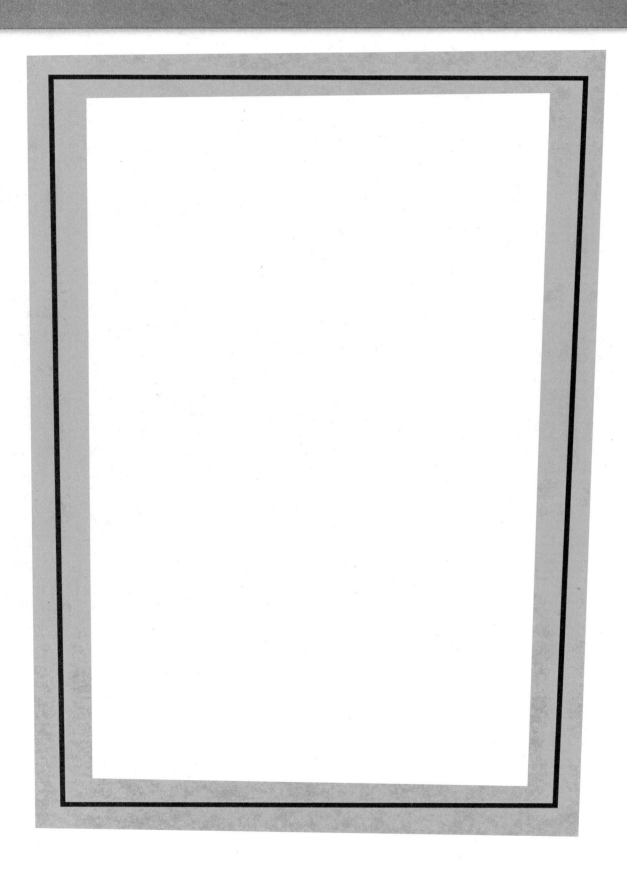